Five Little Monkeys

Chosen by Richard Brown and Kate Ruttle
Illustrated by Martin Chatterton

CAMBRIDGE
UNIVERSITY PRESS

Five little monkeys walked along the shore.

One went a-sailing,

then there were four.

Four little monkeys climbed up a tree.

One tumbled down,
then there were three.

Three little monkeys found a pot of glue.

One got stuck in it,

then there were two.

Two little monkeys found a currant bun.

One ran away with it,

then there was one.

One little monkey cried all afternoon,

so they put him in an aeroplane

and sent him to the moon.

Five little monkeys walked along the shore.
One went a-sailing,
then there were four.
Four little monkeys climbed up a tree.
One tumbled down,
then there were three.
Three little monkeys found a pot of glue.
One got stuck in it,
then there were two.
Two little monkeys found a currant bun.
One ran away with it,
then there was one.
One little monkey cried all afternoon,
so they put him in an aeroplane
and sent him to the moon.